Sophie-Safe Cooking

A Collection of Family Friendly Recipes that are Free of Milk, Eggs, Wheat, Soy, Peanuts, Tree Nuts, Fish, and Shellfish.

Emily Hendrix

I am not a dietician, allergist, or chef. I am a mom, who learned a vast amount while trying to feed my baby. I want to share the knowledge I gained with anyone who it could help. You should consult your allergist about safe ingredients and foods for you and your family, and then this cookbook can help you enjoy your food despite the restrictions.

Nothing in this book constitutes medical advice. The author of this book has no responsibility or liability for use of these recipes, no matter what the consequences. Individuals using the cookbook must verify the safety of ingredients and recipes with an allergist or other doctor.

Illustrations by **Meredith Maddox**
Visit my website at **www.sophiesafecooking.com**

ISBN 978-1-4303-0448-7 – Published by Lulu.com

*For **Sophie**, who needed these recipes so desperately.*

*For **Jeff**, who convinced me that this book could really happen.*

*For **Sharon** and **Michelle**, the chief taste testers.*

*For our **family** and **friends**, who rallied around us,
tasted new foods, and asked the ever-enduring question,*

"Is this Sophie-Safe?"

Chapters & Recipes

Breakfasts

Main Dishes

Side Dishes

Salads

Main Dish Salads

Side Salads

Salad Dressings

Desserts

Sophie's Story

On February 20, 2002, I had my third child, a beautiful baby girl named Sophia Lillian Hendrix. Sophie was healthy and very large—10 pounds, 23 ½ inches at birth. She gave no indication at birth of the health issues to come.

When Sophie was about 3 months old, my husband, Jeff, gave her a taste of a root beer float. Within five minutes, she had hives covering her entire head. I said, "It looks like we have a baby with a milk allergy," as we jumped into the car and headed to the grocery store for Benadryl. At the time, Sophie was still nursing full-time. My pediatrician recommended that I stop eating milk products for 2 weeks and then eat something with milk to see what would happen. From this experiment, it was clear that my dairy intake directly affected Sophie's comfort. When I was eating dairy, she was fussy, gassy, and tended to spit up much more than when I stayed away from it.

As I began to pay more attention to my diet, I realized that Sophie had digestive problems at other times as well. I guessed that these other problems might be due to my diet, and I started noting what I was eating that I thought might cause problems for her. Within a few more months, I had developed a list of suspect allergens: peanuts and eggs, with a few other possibilities. I began cutting these things out of my diet as much as possible.

As Sophie got older, we started to give her baby food. She readily accepted fruits and vegetables, but struggled to keep down oat cereal. At about 8 months, I gave her a bit of bread, and she looked a little rashy later. A few days later, I gave her a piece of flour tortilla and she developed one or two hives around her mouth. At this point I decided it was time to see an allergist for testing. I took Sophie in for scratch testing and she tested positive for allergies to milk, eggs, peanuts, and wheat. Our allergist also told me not to give her any fish, shellfish or other nuts until she was at least 3 years old.

Since I was still nursing Sophie, I stopped eating the things that she is allergic to. At first, I lived on fruits and vegetables, rice, potatoes, and meat. My diet had very little variety and I began to lose weight very quickly. I felt deprived of things I love (such as bread, cookies, and other carbohydrates) and started to feel a little depressed about the situation. As I researched allergy cookbooks, I found the recipes to be strange. Many called for ingredients I had never heard of, and most of them were not very good after all the effort. My family would not eat the things I was making. Out of necessity I began to create my own recipes. Other people started asking for my recipes, and telling me, "you should write a cookbook!"

Sophia (age 2 ½ years) enjoys chocolate cake.

You Can Do This!

When I learned about Sophie's allergies, I felt completely overwhelmed by the responsibility to keep her safe. I did not think that I knew nearly what I needed to know about foods, how things are made, ingredient names; the list goes on and on. I learned how to manage her allergies, and raise a healthy and happy little girl, and you can do the same.

My husband and children agreed that our dinners would all be "Sophie-safe." This was a major help to me in several ways. I felt more supported in my new diet (eliminating allergens). I was also encouraged to be creative and find new ways to prepare old favorites, as well as create new recipes that my family would love. Additionally, as a family we could model the way that Sophie needed to eat, and she would not be eating alone. I encourage you to try to make a similar commitment with those around you. If every dinner is not feasible, try breakfasts or lunch, or a few dinners each week.

In order to change your eating habits, you need support. Find other individuals with allergies, other people in your situation. As you talk with others about your challenges, you will realize that this is not Mission Impossible. 12 million people in the United States live with allergies. They find things to eat. They even enjoy their food. This cookbook will help you do just that!

Customizing Recipes

The purpose of this cookbook is to provide a set of basic recipes that individuals with multiple allergies can utilize. I realize that most people who have more than one food allergy are not allergic to everything excluded from this cookbook. This section will give you the information you need to add ingredients in place of some of the things included in this cookbook.

A recipe is not a prescription for exactly what you must do to make something. A recipe is an idea about how to make a food. It can be thought of as a starting point, which can be altered to meet your family's exact needs. For example, if meatloaf calls for onion, and your family doesn't like onions, leave them out. If you feel it is too bland with the onions left out, mix in some pressed garlic in place of the onions. Recipes with allergens can be altered in much the same way.

Whenever you make substitutions to a recipe, you must expect that it will not work perfectly the first time you make the recipe. It may taste fine, but will probably have a better texture the second or third time you make it as you adjust for your own family's tastes.

Many of the recipes call for margarine or shortening. This should be interpreted as "margarine or shortening that is safe for you." There are many different types of margarine on the market, some of which may not be safe for your allergies. Once you have located specific ingredients that work with your allergies, then you can start working on the recipes.

As an example of how to alter recipes, let's use Apple Muffins. The original recipe reads:

¼ cup	margarine or shortening
⅓ cup	sugar
3 cups	oat flour (see tip on page 3)
½ tsp.	salt
4 tsp.	baking powder
1 cup	rice milk
2 cups	finely chopped apples, such as granny smith
	cinnamon sugar

If you see something in this recipe that you don't like or can't use, simply substitute a similar item for it. Here's the recipe for Apple Muffins with substitutions:

¼ cup	margarine or shortening (any solid fat: butter, lard, etc.)
⅓ cup	sugar
3 cups	oat flour (see tip on page 3)
½ tsp.	salt
4 tsp.	baking powder
1 cup	rice milk (any liquid: soy milk, apple juice, goat's milk, cow's milk, etc.)
2 cups	finely chopped apples, such as granny smith
	cinnamon sugar

A person who has allergies, but is not allergic to milk, could use butter and milk in place of margarine and rice milk if they so desire. When making substitutions, please remember that you have changed the recipe. As such, you may need to make more than one attempt at this "new" recipe in order to perfect it. Don't be afraid to try something new, and don't be afraid to change it a little and try it again!

Breakfasts

Breakfasts

Oatmeal Muffins

1 cup	old-fashioned oats
½ cup	brown sugar
1 tbsp.	apple cider vinegar
1 cup	vanilla rice milk
1 cup	oat flour
2 tsp.	baking powder
½ tsp.	baking soda
½ tsp.	salt
1 tsp.	cinnamon
2 tbsp.	oil

Put oats and brown sugar in a mixing bowl. Pour vinegar and rice milk over top. Allow to soak while mixing other ingredients.

Mix oat flour, baking powder, baking soda, salt and cinnamon in a separate bowl.

Add oil to oat mixture and mix. Add dry ingredients to wet ingredients and mix all together. Pour into muffin pans, using liners, filling each cup about half full.

Bake at 350°F for 20 minutes. Allow to cool for a few minutes in muffin pans before removing, and then enjoy! Makes about 12 muffins.

Oat flour can be purchased at a specialty store, or in the health food section of your local grocery store. However, it is easy and cost-effective to grind your own oats. Simply pour whole oats into your blender and pulse until all of the oats are ground into flour. The oat flour can be stored just as you would store other flours.

Oatmeal Breakfast Cake

Instead of making muffins, use your muffin batter to make a breakfast cake. Make batter as directed in the recipe for Oatmeal Muffins. Pour muffin batter into a greased 8 x 8 baking pan. With a pastry blender, mix:

¼ cup	margarine or shortening (see tip on page *xii*)
2 tbsp.	brown sugar
3 tbsp.	oat flour (see tip on page 3)

Sprinkle the brown sugar mixture over muffin batter.

Bake at 350°F for 25-30 minutes. Allow to cool for 5-10 minutes. Makes 9-12 servings. Cut into squares and enjoy your breakfast cake!

Apple Muffins

These muffins are best when made with a tart apple; granny smith or jonathan are both varieties that work well. Try serving them with apple cider to drink.

¼ cup	margarine or shortening (see tip on page *xii*)
⅓ cup	sugar
3 cups	oat flour (see tip on page 3)
½ tsp.	salt
4 tsp.	baking powder
1 cup	rice milk
2 cups	finely chopped apples, such as granny smith
	cinnamon sugar

Mix margarine or shortening and sugar. Add oat flour, salt, and baking powder. Mix in rice milk. Add apples. Fill lined muffin cups ⅔ full. Sprinkle cinnamon sugar over the batter.

Bake at 400°F for 25 minutes. Makes about 24 muffins.

Oatmeal Pancakes

2 cups	oat flour (see tip on page 3)
2 tbsp.	sugar
½ tsp.	baking soda
½ tsp.	salt
1 ½ tsp.	apple cider vinegar
2 cups	rice milk
2 tbsp.	cooking oil

Mix dry ingredients. Add wet ingredients and mix well. Drop ⅛ cup at a time on hot griddle. Cook until edges dry, and then flip and cook the other side. Makes 24-30 pancakes, 3 inches in diameter.

Add 1 cup fresh or frozen blueberries to the pancake batter. Blueberry pancakes may require a slightly longer cooking time.

Cranberry Bread

1 cup	cranberries, chopped
3 cups	oat flour (*see tip on page 3*)
1 cup	sugar
2 tsp.	baking powder
1 tsp.	salt
½ tsp.	baking soda
2 tbsp.	oil
¾ cup	orange juice
1 ½ tsp.	apple cider vinegar

Mix oat flour, sugar, baking powder, salt, and baking soda. Add juice, oil, and vinegar and mix well. Stir in cranberries by hand. Pour into a greased loaf pan.

Bake at 350°F for 60 minutes. Makes 12 to 18 slices.

Cranberry Muffins

Make Cranberry Bread batter as directed in the recipe above. Spoon batter into lined muffin tins and bake at 350°F for 20 minutes. Makes 18 to 20 muffins.

This makes a great fall treat, and if you choose to make muffins rather than bread, they are easy to take along to the office, school parties, or as a snack.

Banana Bread

2 ½ cups	oat flour (see tip on page 3)
½ cup	sugar
2 tsp.	baking powder
½ tsp.	baking soda
¼ tsp.	salt
3	mashed bananas
¼ cup	margarine or shortening (see tip on page *xii*)
1 tbsp.	apple cider vinegar
3 tbsp.	rice milk

Mix dry ingredients together. Add mashed bananas, margarine or shortening, and rice milk and mix well.

Bake in a greased and sugared loaf pan at 350°F for 60 minutes. Makes 12-18 slices.

To sugar a loaf or cake pan, first grease it with margarine or shortening. Pour 1 tablespoon of white sugar into the loaf pan and turn the pan slowly until the bottom and ½ inch up the sides are coated with sugar.

Tropical Banana Bread

Make Banana Bread batter as directed above, with the following exceptions:

Omit:

	rice milk
Add:	
½ cup	coconut
¾ cup	mandarin oranges, drained.

Bake as directed.

While banana bread is delicious warm, it will be much easier to slice if you allow it to cool first, and then use a bread knife to slice it. When eaten warm, it tends to be more crumbly.

Pumpkin Muffins

I freeze everything—it's much easier to make two and freeze one for later. All of these breads freeze well for a few months. Just make sure to give yourself plenty of time to thaw the breads on the counter (I usually allow mine to thaw overnight)!

2 ⅔ cups	oat flour (see tip on page 3)
1 cup	white sugar
1 tbsp.	baking powder
1 tsp.	cinnamon
¼ tsp.	salt
¼ tsp.	baking soda
¼ tsp.	nutmeg
¼ tsp.	cloves
1 ½ cups	pumpkin, canned
½ cup	rice milk
1 tbsp.	apple cider vinegar
3 tbsp.	vegetable oil

Mix all of the dry ingredients on low speed with a mixer. Add pumpkin, rice milk, vinegar and oil. Mix well. Spoon into lined muffin cups.

Bake at 350°F for 20 minutes. Makes about 18 muffins.

Pumpkin Bread

Prepare Pumpkin Muffin batter as directed in the preceding recipe. Pour batter into a greased bread pan.

Bake at 350°F for 55 minutes. This is delicious pumpkin bread!

Zucchini Bread

2 cups	zucchini, shredded (3-4 zucchini)
¾ cup	sugar
⅓ cup	oil
1 tsp.	vanilla
1 tbsp.	lemon juice
1 tsp.	lemon zest
3 cups	oat flour (see tip on page 3)
1 ½ tsp.	baking powder
¾ tsp.	baking soda
¾ tsp.	salt
1 ½ tsp.	cinnamon
¾ tsp.	cloves

With a mixer, mix zucchini, sugar, oil, vanilla, lemon juice, and lemon zest. Add oat flour, baking powder, baking soda, salt, cinnamon, and cloves. Mix well. Pour into a greased loaf pan.

Bake for 55 minutes at 350°F. Makes 12 to 18 slices.

This recipe works great with fresh or frozen shredded zucchini. To freeze the zucchini, shred it using a cheese grater or your food processor. Measure the shredded zucchini and freeze it in 2 cup portions so that when you thaw it, you can dump it straight into the recipe!

Chocolate Zucchini Muffins

1 ½ cups	zucchini, shredded
½ cup	sugar
¼ cup	oil
1 tsp.	vanilla
1 ½ tsp.	apple cider vinegar
¼ cup	rice milk
2 cups	oat flour (see tip on page 3)
⅓ cup	cocoa powder
1 tsp.	baking powder
½ tsp.	baking soda
½ tsp.	salt
2 tbsp.	cinnamon

Mix zucchini, sugar, oil, vanilla, vinegar, and rice milk. Add oat flour, cocoa powder, baking powder, baking soda, salt, and cinnamon and mix until combined. Spoon into lined muffin cups.

Bake at 350°F for 20 minutes. Makes 12 muffins.

Blueberry-Banana Smoothie

In a blender or smoothie machine combine:

2 cups	frozen blueberries
2	frozen bananas
3 cups	rice milk
½ tbsp.	lemon juice

This makes a very thick, very cold smoothie. If you prefer a thinner smoothie, try using fresh bananas rather than frozen. Makes about 4 cups.

Strawberry Smoothie

Smoothies are a great option for a quick, satisfying breakfast or a snack, especially because all of the ingredients can be easily kept on hand. When your fresh bananas start to brown, simply toss them in the freezer, peels and all. To use them in a smoothie, run the whole banana under warm tap water for a few seconds and peel it, then break the frozen banana into 2 or 3 chunks and toss it in the blender!

In a blender or smoothie machine combine:

3 cups	frozen strawberries
3 cups	rice milk
⅓ cup	sugar or honey

This smoothie is similar to a strawberry shake. Makes about 4 cups.

Main Dishes

Main Dishes

Chicken Strips

Rounded out with Oven Fries and a green salad, this makes a very satisfying meal for adults and kids alike.

3	boneless, skinless chicken breasts, cut into strips
1 cup	crushed plain potato chips
2 tsp.	garlic pepper blend
1 tsp.	salt
2 tsp.	dried parsley

Mix all ingredients except for the chicken. Roll chicken strips in dry mixture. If chicken is too dry for the mixture to stick to it, dip the strips in water before rolling in potato chip mixture.

Bake on a lightly greased cookie sheet for 16 minutes at 450°F. Serves 4.

Kielbasa Stew

1 can	tomato sauce (15 oz.)
4 cups	water
2 cans	great northern beans (15.5 oz.), rinsed and drained
1 ½ lbs.	kielbasa, cut into small chunks
6 cups	potatoes, cubed
2 cups	carrots, cubed
¾ tsp.	dried thyme
¼ tsp.	fresh ground pepper
2	bay leaves

Place all ingredients in a large pot. Bring to a boil and simmer 20 minutes or until potatoes and carrots are tender.

Makes 8 to 10 servings.

This stew is great the day after, and tastes great having been frozen. Make your life easier and make enough for a second meal later.

Chicken Soup with Rice

2 cups	cooked, chopped chicken
5 cups	chicken broth
1 cup	rice, uncooked
	salt
	pepper

Put chicken, chicken broth and rice in a large saucepan. Add salt and pepper to taste.

Bring to boiling and simmer until rice is soft. Serve immediately. Makes about 6 servings.

With the right preparations, this meal can be on the table in 15 minutes. Simply use canned or frozen chicken broth, and rice leftover from another meal. Dump everything in the pot and heat through.

Quick Beef-Vegetable Soup

For a little variety, add extra water and 1 cup rice, and then simmer until rice is done. Adjust spices to taste.

1 lb.	ground beef, browned
16 oz.	frozen mixed vegetables
2	bay leaves
2 tsp.	salt
¼ tsp.	pepper
1 tsp.	oregano
½ tsp.	marjoram
	water to barely cover

Bring to a boil and simmer for 20 minutes to blend flavors. Makes 4 servings.

Mexican Beef with Rice

Brown:

1 lb.	ground beef
2 cloves	garlic, pressed

Mix with:

2 ½ cups	rice, uncooked
5 cups	water
1 can	tomato sauce (15 oz.)
1 tbsp.	chili powder
1 tsp.	cumin
1 tsp.	salt
¼ tsp.	pepper

Cook in rice cooker (not steamer) or on stovetop until rice is done (about 30 minutes). Makes 8 servings, ¾ cup each.

Serve with:
Avocados, sliced
Lettuce, shredded
Tomatoes, chopped
Corn chips
Corn tortillas

Beef Soft Tacos

Brown:

1 lb.	ground beef

With:

2 or 3 cloves	garlic, pressed
1 tbsp.	chili powder
1 tsp.	salt
¼ tsp.	pepper
1 tsp.	cumin

Makes 6 servings.

Serve with:
Corn tortillas
Avocado, sliced
Shredded lettuce
Salsa
Beans
Rice
Whipped beans
Corn

Chicken Soft Tacos

Cut into thin strips:

1 lb.	boneless, skinless chicken breasts

Heat over medium:

2 tbsp.	oil

Cook chicken 10-15 minutes, until no longer pink.

While cooking, add:

¾ tsp.	salt
2 tsp.	chili powder
1 tsp.	cumin
¼ tsp.	pepper
2 cloves	garlic, pressed

Makes 6 servings.

Serve with:
Corn tortillas
Avocado, sliced
Shredded lettuce
Salsa
Beans
Rice
Whipped beans
Corn

Potato Corn Chowder

¼ cup	onion, chopped
¼ cup	green pepper, chopped
¼ cup	red sweet pepper, chopped
3 tbsp.	oil
6	medium russet potatoes, peeled and diced
2 cups	frozen corn
2 tsp.	salt

Saute onion and green pepper in oil until tender. Add potatoes and enough water to barely cover. Cook until tender (about 20 minutes).

Add corn and salt. Heat until corn is thoroughly warm.

To thicken soup, put 1 cup of soup in the blender and puree. Add pureed soup back to pot and cook for one more minute.

Makes 6 servings.

A quick and simple meal perfect for a cold day, or an alternative to mashed potatoes for a fancier dinner.

Shepherd's Pie

1 lb.	ground beef, browned
1 tsp.	salt
1 can	green beans (14.5 oz.), drained
1 can	corn (15.25 oz.), drained
1 can	tomato sauce (15 oz.)
	mashed potatoes (see recipe in Side Dishes)

Mix and heat all ingredients except mashed potatoes in a skillet. Spread mixture on the bottom of a 9 x 13 pan.

Top with about 6 servings of mashed potatoes. (You can dollop spoonfuls of mashed potatoes on the meat mixture, or spread the mashed potatoes evenly over the entire pan.) Sprinkle paprika over the mashed potatoes.

Bake at 400°F for about 25 minutes or until meat mixture is bubbly and potatoes begin to brown slightly. Makes 9 to 12 servings.

Mary Alice's Zucchini and Rice

1 lb.	ground beef
¼ cup	minced onion
¾ tsp.	salt
	fresh ground pepper
1 tsp.	allspice
5	zucchini, sliced
1 can	tomato sauce (15 oz.)
4 cups	rice, cooked

Brown ground beef with onion and spices. Add zucchini. Cover and cook until zucchini are soft.

Mix in tomato sauce and heat through. Serve over rice. Makes 6 servings.

This delicious meal conveniently uses up those extra zucchini from the garden.

Beef Pot Roast

2-3 lb.	pot roast
2 tbsp.	oil
1 ½ cups	water
2 tsp.	salt
½ tsp.	freshly ground black pepper
1 tsp.	dried basil
4	medium potatoes
8	small carrots
2 stalks	celery

Heat oil in a skillet over high heat. Brown roast in hot oil. Slice potatoes, carrots, and celery and lay on the bottom of slow cooker.

Place browned roast on top. Sprinkle salt, pepper, and basil over roast. Pour water over the roast and vegetables. Cook in slow cooker on low for 8 hours or on high for 4 hours. Makes 6 servings.

You can also make gravy with the drippings from the roast by following the gravy directions included with Easy Roasted Chicken and Gravy.

Pork Roast

6	russet potatoes (or another variety you like)
2 lb.	pork roast
2 tsp.	sage
2 tsp.	salt
1/4 tsp.	freshly ground black pepper
1 cup	apple juice

Slice potatoes and layer them on the bottom of a slow cooker.

Place roast on top of potatoes. Sprinkle with sage, salt and pepper. Pour apple juice over roast.

Cook on low for 8 hours or high for 4 hours. Makes 6 servings.

You can also make gravy with the drippings from the roast by following the gravy directions included with Easy Roasted Chicken and Gravy.

Easy Roasted Chicken and Gravy

1	whole chicken
2 cloves	garlic
1 tsp.	rosemary or 3-4 sprigs fresh rosemary
	salt and pepper to taste

Remove organs and neck from chicken cavity and discard. Press garlic and rub inside chicken cavity. Sprinkle salt, pepper, and rosemary inside cavity. (If using fresh rosemary, place sprigs inside chicken.)

Place in a slow cooker and cook on low for 8 hours or on high for 4 hours. Makes 6 servings.

Roast Gravy

2 cups	liquid (see below)
2 tbsp.	corn starch
1 tbsp.	margarine or shortening (see tip on page *xii*)
	salt and pepper

Remove chicken from slow cooker and pour liquid into a 2-cup measuring cup. If necessary, add water to make 2 cups total liquid.

In a small saucepan, melt margarine or shortening over medium heat. Mix in corn starch. Add liquid and heat to boiling, stirring often.

Boil about 1 minute to thicken. Add salt and pepper to taste.

Granny's Meatloaf

2 lbs.	ground beef
1 lb.	pork sausage
1	onion, chopped
½	green pepper, chopped
1 cup	tomato sauce
1 ½ tsp.	salt
8	medium new potatoes, halved or quartered
4	small onions
4	carrots, halved or quartered
	salt
	fresh ground pepper

Mix ground beef, sausage, onion, green pepper, tomato sauce, and salt. Form into a loaf shape in the center of a 9 x 13 pan.

Place potatoes, onions, and carrots around meatloaf. Sprinkle salt and pepper on vegetables. Cover with aluminum foil.

Bake at 350°F for 90 minutes. Uncover and bake 30 more minutes. You may top the meatloaf with more tomato sauce if desired.

This recipe serves at least 8 people. I recommend removing half of the meatloaf when finished cooking and freezing it for a later meal.

Porcupine Meatballs

1 can	tomato sauce (15 oz.)
¼ cup	rice, uncooked
1 tsp.	minced dried onion
1 clove	garlic, pressed
¼ tsp.	pepper
¼ tsp.	dry mustard
1 tsp.	apple cider vinegar
1 lb.	ground beef
½ tsp.	dried oregano
1 tsp.	salt
4 cups	cooked rice

Mix ⅓ cup of tomato sauce, ¼ cup rice, uncooked, onion, garlic, pepper, mustard, vinegar and ground beef. Shape into 20 meatballs. Place in large skillet.

Mix remaining sauce, oregano, salt, and ½ cup water. Pour over meatballs.

Bring to boiling, reduce heat and cover. Allow to simmer for 20 minutes or until rice and meat are both done. Serve over rice. Makes 4 servings.

If you are making a bigger batch, the meatballs can be put in one or more 9 x 13 pans, covered with foil, and baked at 375°F for 20 minutes. These can be frozen, but they usually crumble after thawing. They still taste great, they're just not perfect for presentation.

Pantry Chili

This chili is almost completely made up of things that could typically be found in the pantry.

1 lb.	ground beef
1 tbsp.	chili powder
2 tbsp.	brown sugar
1 tsp.	salt
3 cloves	garlic, pressed
1 tsp.	cumin
1 tbsp.	dry onions
1 can	black beans (15 oz.), rinsed and drained
1 can	corn (15.25 oz.), drained
1 can	pinto beans, rinsed and drained
1 can	tomato sauce (15 oz.)
	fresh cilantro

Brown ground beef with spices and garlic. Add beans, corn and tomato sauce.

Simmer for 10 minutes to heat all ingredients thoroughly.

Serve over corn bread or baked potatoes. Garnish with fresh cilantro. Makes 6 servings.

Melanie's Spaghetti Sauce

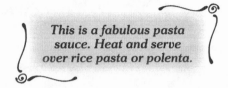

This is a fabulous pasta sauce. Heat and serve over rice pasta or polenta.

1 lb.	ground beef
1 tsp.	olive oil
1 can	tomato sauce (15 oz.)
⅔ cup	water
¼ can	tomato paste (6 oz)
1 tsp.	sugar
¼	carrot, grated
1 tsp.	dried basil
	fresh ground pepper
	salt to taste

In a large pot, brown ground beef and drain excess fat. Add olive oil, tomato sauce, water, tomato paste, sugar, carrot, pepper and basil.

Simmer for 30 minutes, or longer if you have time. Just before serving, add salt and margarine or olive oil. Makes 5 servings.

Chicken Vegetable Soup

2 cups	cooked and cubed or shredded chicken
4 cups	chicken broth
16 oz.	frozen vegetable (peas, carrots, corn, etc.)
1	bay leaf
	salt and pepper to taste

Place all ingredients in a soup pot. Cover and cook until completely heated throughout, about 15 minutes. Makes 4 servings.

For variety, add 1 cup cooked rice or other grain, such as pasta, barley, etc.

Lentil Stew

1 ½ cups	lentils
6 cups	water
2 cloves	garlic, pressed or minced
½ cup	celery, chopped
1 ½ cups	carrots, chopped
⅓ cup	onion, minced
⅛ tsp.	dried thyme
2 tsp.	salt
2 tsp.	lemon juice

Place lentils and water in a pot. Bring to a boil and reduce heat to simmer for 60 minutes.

Add garlic, celery, carrots, onion, thyme, and salt and simmer 20 minutes more. Add lemon juice just before serving. Makes 4 to 6 servings.

Middle Eastern Chili

1 lb.	ground lamb
1 small	eggplant, diced
1	onion, chopped
1 small	green pepper, chopped
1-8oz.	can stewed tomatoes
1 tsp.	curry powder
½ tsp.	allspice
½ tsp.	nutmeg
¼ tsp.	garlic powder
	fresh cilantro

Brown the lamb and drain the excess fat. Add eggplant, onion, and pepper. Cook 2-3 minutes, until onion softens.

Add tomatoes, curry powder, allspice, nutmeg and garlic powder and simmer until eggplant is soft. Serve with fresh cilantro as a garnish. Makes 4 servings.

Tantalizing alone, this chili can also be served over rice.

Stuffed Green Peppers

2 large	green peppers
1 lb.	ground beef or sausage
⅓ cup	chopped onion
1 ½ cups	tomato sauce
⅓ cup	rice
1 tsp.	salt
1 tsp.	vinegar
½ tsp.	dried basil
¼ tsp.	pepper

Cut peppers in half lengthwise. Remove seeds, stems and membranes. Immerse in boiling water for 3 minutes. After removing, sprinkle with salt and allow to drain on paper towels.

Brown meat and onion. Drain excess fat, and then add tomato sauce, ½ cup water, rice, salt, vinegar, basil, and pepper. Bring to boiling and simmer until rice is done.

Place peppers in an 8 x 8 baking dish and fill with meat mixture. Bake at 375°F for 15 minutes. Makes 4 servings.

Baked Potato Soup

2 cloves	garlic, pressed
1 tbsp.	oil
6	russet potatoes, peeled or very clean and cubed
2 tsp.	salt
	ground pepper to taste

Sauté garlic in oil for 1 minute. Add potatoes, salt, and enough water to barely cover. Bring to a boil and simmer for about 20 minutes, or until potatoes are tender.

Mash slightly with a potato masher, leaving lots of chunks of potato. Top each bowl with any combination of:

Crumbled Bacon
Chives
Steamed Broccoli

Makes 6 servings.

Baked Potato Bar

6-8 baking potatoes
Pantry Chili
steamed broccoli
bacon
Melanie's Spaghetti Sauce
Creamed Chicken and Peas

Scrub baking potatoes. Dry potatoes, prick with a fork, and bake at 400°F for 45 to 60 minutes. Serve with various topping options listed above.

This is a great way to use up leftovers from other meals. This meal also works well with children, since they often change their tastes. With this recipe, they can choose which things to eat.

Creamed Chicken and Peas

2 tbsp.	oil
2 tbsp.	corn starch
¼ tsp.	black pepper
3 cups	chicken broth
2 cups	shredded chicken
½ cup	frozen peas

Mix oil, corn starch, and pepper in a saucepan. Begin heating over medium heat. Add chicken broth all at once.

Stir over medium heat until boiling. Heat about 2 more minutes, until sauce is thick. Add chicken and peas. Serve over rice or potatoes. Makes 6 servings.

Tamale Pie

Beef Layer:

1 lb.	ground beef
1 can	tomato sauce (15 oz.)
1 can	corn (15.25 oz.), drained
2 cloves	garlic
¼ tsp.	fresh ground black pepper
1 tsp.	cumin
1 tbsp.	chili powder
1 tsp.	salt

Brown ground beef. Add other ingredients and simmer for a few minutes to blend flavors. While beef mixture is simmering, mix corn bread layer.

Corn Bread Layer:

1 ¼ cups	corn meal
1 ¼ cups	oat flour (see tip on page 3)
¼ cup	sugar
2 tsp.	baking powder
½ tsp.	baking soda
½ tsp.	salt
1 ¼ cups	rice milk
1 tsp.	apple cider vinegar
3 tbsp.	oil

Mix all of the dry ingredients. Add rice milk and oil and mix well.

Pour beef mixture into a 9 x 13 pan. Top with corn bread mixture and bake at 400°F for 25 to 30 minutes, until a knife or toothpick placed in the corn bread mixture comes out clean. Makes 9 to 12 servings.

Mom's Best Beef Stew

2 lbs.	stew beef
2 tbsp.	corn starch
⅛ tsp.	salt
dash of	pepper

Brown the stew beef in a skillet over high heat. Use bacon grease if available. Sprinkle the meat with the corn starch, salt and pepper. Then add:

2 cloves	garlic, pressed
1	large onion, chopped
1 cup	beef or chicken broth
1 cup	tomato sauce
12	whole peppercorns
3	whole cloves
¼ cup	chopped parsley
⅓	bay leaf

Cover and simmer meat and seasonings for 2-3 hours or until meat is tender. In a separate pot, place:

6	medium sized potatoes, peeled or very clean and quartered
6	medium sized carrots, peeled and quartered
1	rib of celery, chopped

Barely cover vegetables with water and cook until nearly tender. Add to the beef mixture and cook together for 15 minutes before serving. Makes 6 to 8 servings.

My husband calls this "Christmas stew" because the smell of the cloves simmering reminds him of wassail. Despite the nickname, we eat it all year long.

Chicken and Squash Goulash

1 tbsp.	oil
2	boneless skinless chicken breasts, cubed
5 small	yellow summer squash, thinly sliced
2 cloves	garlic, pressed or diced
¼ tsp.	fresh ground black pepper
1 tsp.	salt
2-3 tbsp.	chopped fresh basil
1 can	tomato sauce (15 oz.)
1 ½ cups	rice
3 cups	water

Heat oil in a large skillet with a lid. When oil is hot, add chicken breasts and garlic and cook 5 minutes while slicing squash.

Add sliced squash, pepper, salt and basil. Cook about 10 minutes with the lid on the skillet, stirring every 2-3 minutes.

When chicken is completely cooked, add tomato sauce, rice, and water. Replace lid. Bring to a boil, then reduce to a simmer and cook until rice is done. Makes 6 servings.

Split Pea Soup

2 cups	split peas
2 quarts	water
1	ham bone
1 cup	celery, chopped
¼ cup	onion, chopped
1 ½ cups	carrots, diced
1	bay leaf
¼ tsp.	thyme
	salt
	pepper

Wash peas and sort out any odd looking peas or stones. Add water. Bring to a boil and simmer for 2 minutes. Remove from heat.

Allow to sit covered for 1 hour. Add all other ingredients except salt and pepper. Bring to a boil and simmer for 2 ½ to 3 hours.

Remove ham bone. Cut meat off bone, dice and return meat to soup. Season with salt and pepper and serve. Makes 8 servings.

Chicken Continental

1 ½ cups	chicken breast, cooked and cubed
1 can	mushrooms, drained
1 clove	garlic, pressed
2 tbsp.	oil
1 can	green beans (14.5 oz.), undrained
1 tsp.	salt
½ tsp.	basil
dash of	pepper
1 ½ cups	rice
1 can	chicken broth (13.75 oz.)

Saute chicken, mushrooms, and garlic in oil for 2 to 3 minutes. Add remaining ingredients and bring to a full boil. Reduce heat to simmer until rice is cooked. Makes 6 servings.

This is one of those quick and easy meals that even includes a green vegetable. If you use canned chicken for the chicken breast, then all of the ingredients can be kept on hand in the pantry. Now that's simple!

Sausage Potato Scramble

This is an absolute favorite. I remember loving it when I was a child, and my children request it on a regular basis. To lighten it up, use light or turkey sausage. We always serve it with an apple dish, either Apple Sauté, or plain old applesauce from a jar.

12-16 oz.	bulk breakfast sausage
1	onion, minced
6-8	medium russet potatoes, peeled and cut into bite-sized chunks
3 tbsp.	margarine or shortening (see tip on page *xii*)
2 tbsp.	corn starch
1 ½ to 2 cups	chicken broth

In a large pot, put potatoes and enough water to barely cover them. Bring to a boil and then simmer potatoes until they are tender. When the potatoes are tender, drain the liquid.

While potatoes are cooking, brown sausage and onion. Drain the grease off of the sausage and mix in margarine or shortening and corn starch.

Over low heat, add chicken broth and potatoes and stir gently until mixture is thick. Makes 6 to 8 servings.

Kim's Black Eyed Pea Soup

1 ¼ cups	black eyed peas
2 tbsp.	vegetable oil
½	onion, chopped
1 tsp.	minced garlic
1 cup	green pepper, chopped
5 cups	chicken broth
1	bay leaf
1 tsp.	salt
¼ tsp.	red pepper flakes
¾ cup	smoked turkey, diced
	cilantro

Soak peas overnight in cold water. Drain, rinse, and drain again.

Saute onion and garlic in oil. Add peas, pepper, broth, bay leaf, salt, and red pepper flakes. Bring to a boil and reduce heat to simmer for 1 hour. Stir in turkey and simmer for 15 minutes more.

Garnish with cilantro.

Makes 6 servings.

Chicken Enchiladas

For the enchiladas:

12 to 16	corn tortillas
1 ½ cups	chicken, cooked and shredded
1 cup	whipped or refried beans
1 can	green chilies (4 oz.), divided
1 can	corn (15.25 oz.), drained

In a mixing bowl, stir together chicken, beans, ⅔ of the can of green chilies, and corn. Put a large spoonful of the chicken mixture in the center of each tortilla. Roll the tortilla around the chicken and place in a 9 x 13 pan.

For the sauce:

1 tbsp.	margarine or oil
2 cloves	garlic
2 tbsp.	corn starch
¼ tsp.	pepper
2 cups	chicken broth
½ tsp.	salt
⅓ can	green chilies

In a small saucepan, heat margarine or oil over medium heat. Press the garlic with a garlic press into the oil and cook for 1 minute. Whisk cornstarch and pepper into oil and garlic. Add chicken broth and salt and whisk together. Stir frequently while bringing the sauce to a boil. Cook the sauce for 1 more minute once it is boiling. Remove the sauce from the heat and add remaining ⅓ can of green chilies.

Pour the sauce over the enchiladas. Bake uncovered at 375°F for 30 minutes or until the enchiladas are hot and tortillas are slightly browned. Makes 6 to 8 servings of 2 enchiladas each. Garnish with fresh chopped tomatoes and cilantro.

Put the corn tortillas in a plastic bag and heat in the microwave for 1 to 2 minutes. This will make them more pliable.

Spicy Chicken Bake

2	boneless skinless chicken breasts
1 can	tomato sauce (15 oz.)
1 can	green chilies (4 oz.)
1 cup	white rice
2 cups	hot water
1 can	corn (15.25 oz.), drained
1 can	black beans (15 oz.), rinsed and drained
2 tsp.	salt
¼ tsp.	black pepper
1 tsp.	cumin
3 cloves	garlic

Put all ingredients except chicken breasts into a 9 x 13 pan and mix together.

Trim chicken breasts and place on top of rice mixture. Cover and bake at 375°F for 1 hour 20 minutes, or until chicken is cooked through and all liquid is absorbed.

Side Dishes

Side Dishes

Mashed Potatoes

Dice:

6-8	medium potatoes, scrubbed clean or peeled

Add water to barely cover. Bring to a boil and then simmer until very soft—about 20 minutes. Drain potatoes, reserving cooking liquid. Mash, adding:

1 cup	reserved liquid
½ cup	margarine or olive oil
1 ½ tsp.	salt
	fresh ground black pepper

Add more liquid as needed to reach desired texture. Serves 6.

You can boil the potatoes in chicken broth instead of water. In this case, adjust the amount of salt to taste.

Garlic Mashed Potatoes

6-8	medium russet potatoes
3 cloves	garlic
1 tsp.	salt
	fresh ground pepper
¼ cup	margarine or olive oil

Peel and dice potatoes. Peel garlic cloves. Put potatoes and garlic in a pot. Add enough water to barely cover potatoes and boil until tender, about 15 minutes. Drain potatoes, saving the liquid. Remove garlic cloves and, using a garlic press, add back into potatoes. Mash potatoes using a potato masher or mixer, adding salt, pepper, margarine or olive oil, and reserved liquid until desired consistency and flavor is achieved.

Corn Bread

1 ¼ cups	corn meal
1 ¼ cups	oat flour (see tip on page 3)
½ cup	sugar
2 tsp.	baking powder
½ tsp.	baking soda
½ tsp.	salt
1 ¼ cups	rice milk
3 tbsp.	oil
1 tbsp.	apple cider vinegar

Mix all of the dry ingredients. Add rice milk, oil, and vinegar and mix well. Pour into a greased 8 x 8 pan.

Bake at 400°F for 25 minutes. Serves 9.

Corn Muffins

Make batter according to Corn Bread recipe above. Instead of using an 8 x 8 pan, put liners in a muffin pan and fill each cup ⅔ full of corn bread batter.

Bake for 20 minutes at 400°F. Makes 10-12 corn muffins.

Fiesta Corn Bread

1 ¼ cups	corn meal
1 ¼ cups	oat flour (see tip on page 3)
½ cup	sugar
2 tsp.	baking powder
½ tsp.	baking soda
½ tsp.	salt
1 tbsp.	apple cider vinegar
⅔ cup	rice milk
4 tsp.	dry onion
¼ cup	chopped red bell pepper
1 can	chopped green chilies (4 oz.)
½ cup	oil
1 can	creamed corn (15.5 oz.)

Mix corn meal, oat flour, sugar, baking powder, baking soda, and salt.

Add vinegar, rice milk, onion, red pepper, green chilies, oil, and creamed corn. Mix well. Pour the batter into a greased 9 x 9 baking dish.

Cook at 400°F for 55 minutes. Serves 9.

For a little more kick, try replacing the green chilies with 1-2 tbsp. of chopped jalapeno peppers.

Oven Fries

6-8	medium potatoes, scrubbed clean or peeled
2 tbsp.	oil
2 tsp.	salt
¾ tsp.	ground black pepper

Cut potatoes into quarters lengthwise. Toss with oil, salt and pepper.

Bake on a greased cookie sheet at 400°F for 45 minutes. Stir potatoes every 15 minutes while baking. Serves 6.

In addition to salt and pepper, add 2 tsp. dried rosemary or use garlic salt in place of salt, pepper and rosemary.

Sweet Potato Fries

4	sweet potatoes
2-3 tbsp.	oil
	salt and pepper to taste
¼ tsp.	cayenne pepper (optional)

Peel and slice sweet potatoes. Put oil, salt and pepper in a resealable plastic bag, add potatoes and shake to coat.

Spread sweet potatoes on a non-stick baking pan or greased cookie sheet and bake 45 minutes at 400°F.

Mary Alice's Garlic Hummus

1 can	garbanzo beans, rinsed and drained
1 tbsp.	olive oil
4 tbsp.	lemon juice
2 cloves	garlic, pressed
¼ tsp.	salt
¼ tsp.	cayenne pepper
¼ cup	liquid from beans

Put beans, olive oil, lemon juice, garlic, salt and cayenne pepper in food processor and blend until smooth. Add reserved bean liquid a little at a time until the hummus reaches the consistency that you like. It will keep in the refrigerator for up to 1 week. Serve with carrots, celery, corn chips, or use your imagination! This recipe makes about 2 cups.

Mix in one of the following: Roasted red pepper, chopped sun-dried tomatoes, or chopped jalapenos.

Summer Squash with Basil

If you can get your hands on some, this is even more delicious with lemon basil.

1 tbsp.	oil
3	medium summer squash or zucchini, thinly sliced
20	basil leaves, roughly chopped
½ tsp.	salt

Cook oil over medium heat until hot. Add squash, basil and salt. Stir. Turn heat to low and cook about 10-15 minutes until squash is soft. Serves 4.

Margaret's Garden Special

1 tbsp.	oil
3 or 4	small zucchini, sliced
1 can	corn (15.25 oz.), drained
1 small	green pepper, chopped
1 or 2	fresh tomatoes, diced
	salt and pepper to taste

Over medium heat, heat oil in a pan large enough to hold all of the ingredients. Add the vegetables one at a time, creating layers; zucchini first, then corn, then pepper, with the tomatoes on the top. Add salt and pepper to taste. With the cover on, cook vegetables for about 15 minutes, or until the zucchini is soft.

For a more southwestern feel, substitute a hot pepper, finely diced, or 2 tbsp. chopped green chilies for the green pepper and leave out the tomatoes.

Whipped Pinto Beans

2 ½ cups	dry pinto beans
	water
1 tsp.	baking soda
1 tsp.	cumin powder
	lime juice
	salt
	cilantro

Soak overnight in 1 quart of water with 1 tsp. baking soda.

Put 8 cups water, 2 tsp. salt, and 1 tsp. cumin powder in a large pot. Bring water to a boil. Add drained beans. Simmer beans for about 2 hours or until very soft.

After simmering, drain and save the liquid from the beans. Puree the beans, adding reserved liquid as necessary to make the consistency that you prefer. Add lime juice, salt and cilantro to taste. Makes about 6 cups.

Steamed Vegetables

Many of the side dishes we eat are as simple as steaming vegetables and adding a little flavoring. Vegetables can be steamed in a steamer (see the directions for yours) or a covered dish in a microwave with a little water at the bottom of the dish.

A few favorites are:

Broccoli with lemon juice
Cauliflower
Asparagus with vinaigrette
Brussel Sprouts with lemon juice
Winter Squash with brown sugar and margarine

Baconed Green Beans

5 cups	water
3 cups	fresh green beans
3 slices	bacon, cooked and crumbled
1 tsp.	salt
¼ tsp.	black pepper

Bring water to a boil. Add remaining ingredients. Simmer for 20-25 minutes, until green beans are slightly soft. To serve, drain most of the liquid, but leave the bacon with the green beans. Serves 6.

Baked Sweet Potatoes

6-8 large sweet potatoes

Wash the skins. Prick with a fork. Place on a cookie sheet.

Bake at 400°F for 45 to 60 minutes. Serve with margarine and brown sugar or cinnamon sugar. Serves 6 to 8.

Nachos

Corn chips	
2 cups	whipped beans
½ lb.	ground beef
½ lb.	bulk sausage
1 tsp.	salt
2 cloves	garlic
	diced tomatoes
	green chilies
	black olives
	fresh cilantro
	limes

Brown ground beef and sausage with garlic and salt. Add whipped beans and mix well. Spread corn chips on a cookie sheet.

Drop spoonfuls of bean and meat mixture all over the chips.

Bake in a 350°F oven for 10 minutes, long enough to warm all ingredients. Immediately top with tomatoes, green chilies, olives, and cilantro and garnish with limes. Serve warm. Serves 10.

Guacamole

2	very ripe avocados
½ tsp.	salt
¼ tsp.	black pepper
1 tbsp.	lime juice
2 tbsp.	chopped fresh cilantro
1 can	chopped green chilies (4 oz.)

Mash avocados with a fork or potato masher. Mix in salt, pepper, lime juice, cilantro, and green chilies. Serve with corn chips. Makes 1 ½ to 2 cups.

When using avocados, cut the fruit in half lengthwise around the pit. Twist slightly to separate the two halves. Cut each half again and simply peel the skin off the flesh.

Southwestern Beans

2 ½ cups	pinto beans (soaked according to package directions)
12 cups	water
4 tsp.	salt
1 tbsp.	chili powder
½ tsp.	cayenne pepper
2 tsp.	cumin
½ tsp.	black pepper
4-5 cloves	garlic, pressed

Bring water to a boil. Add beans and seasonings and bring back to a boil. Simmer for 2 hours or until beans are soft. Serve as a side dish or as a taco topping. Makes about 6 cups.

Apple Sauté

If your apples are too sweet, add a little lemon juice. If they are too tart, add a little sugar. A little goes a long way, so don't add more than ½ teaspoon at a time.

3 or 4	apples, peeled (if desired) and sliced
1 tbsp.	oil
1 tsp.	cinnamon
	sugar (optional)
	lemon juice (optional)

Heat oil in a skillet over medium heat until hot. Place apple slices in the skillet. Sprinkle the cinnamon on top and cook for 15 to 20 minutes or until apples are soft but still hold their shape.

Salads

Salads

Main Dish Salads

Side Salads

Salad Dressings

Bacon Potato Salad

Boil 8 to 10 Yukon Gold potatoes (or substitute an equal amount of another potato that you like) for 25 minutes.

While potatoes are boiling, whisk together the following ingredients:

¼ cup	oil
⅛ cup	apple cider vinegar
⅛ cup	water
1 tbsp.	sugar
1 tsp.	mustard
2 tsp.	dry parsley
1 tsp.	salt
	fresh ground pepper to taste

Rinse potatoes in cold water. Peel and slice into a large bowl. Pour dressing over potatoes while they are still warm. Add ½ cup (or more) crumbled bacon. Stir together and serve warm or cold. Makes 5 main dish servings.

Potato Salad with Kielbasa

6	medium russet potatoes

Peel and cube potatoes. Boil, barely covered in water, for 15 minutes or until tender.

While potatoes boil, whisk together:

3 tbsp.	apple cider vinegar
1 ½ tsp.	dry mustard
1 tsp.	dill
¼ cup	apple juice
¼ cup	oil
	salt and pepper to taste

Drain potatoes and place in a large bowl. Sprinkle salt and pepper over potatoes.

Add half of the dressing and:

2	green onions, chopped
¾ lb.	kielbasa, cut into small pieces and boiled for 5 min.

Serve over:

	Romaine lettuce, washed and chopped

Add reserved dressing as needed. Makes 6 main dish servings.

Taco Salad

Meat:

1 lb.	ground beef
2 cloves	garlic, pressed
1 tbsp.	chili powder
¾ tsp.	salt
1 tsp.	cumin
¼ tsp.	freshly ground black pepper
3 tbsp.	water

Brown ground beef and garlic in skillet. Drain fat. Add spices and water. Simmer for a few minutes to blend flavors.

Salad:

1 head	lettuce
1 can	corn (15.25 oz.), drained
1	avocado, cubed
2	tomatoes, cubed
4	green onions, chopped

Meat mixture:

1 can	black beans (15 oz.), rinsed and drained

Layer ingredients in a large bowl and toss just before serving.

Serve with corn chips if desired. Use Taco Vinaigrette for dressing. Makes 6 main dish servings.

Mandarin Chicken Salad

1 bunch	romaine lettuce, torn or chopped
2 stalks	celery, diced
2	green onions, chopped
1 can	mandarin oranges (8 oz.), drained
2 cups	cooked, chopped chicken

Mix all ingredients. Serve with Sweet and Sour Vinaigrette. Makes 6 main dish servings.

Curried Rice Salad

This salad is great with brown or wild rice instead of plain white rice!

Dressing:

¼ cup	oil
2 tbsp.	honey
2 tbsp.	lime juice
2 tbsp.	apple cider vinegar
1 tsp.	salt
1 tsp.	curry (or more per your tastes)

Mix all ingredients in a small bowl with a wire whisk.

Salad:

4 cups	cooked rice
8 oz. can	mandarin oranges, drained
1 cup	red grapes, halved
½ cup	celery, sliced into thin pieces
1 cup	granny smith apple, diced
1 cup	pineapple tidbits, drained
3 cups	cooked, diced chicken or canned chicken

Put all ingredients in a large mixing bowl. Pour dressing over top and mix together. Serve cold or warm. Makes 6 to 8 main dish servings.

Southwestern Green Salad

4 cups	mixed lettuce
1 bunch	cilantro
2	tomatoes
1	green pepper
2-3	green onions, chopped

Tear lettuce into bite-sized pieces. Tear cilantro leaves off of the stems, keeping leaves whole. Chop tomatoes into small pieces. Chop green pepper into small pieces. Add all ingredients together and toss. Serve with Taco Vinaigrette. Serves 5.

Fruit Salad

1 cup	grapes, halved
1 cup	oranges, peeled and diced
1 cup	pineapple, diced
1 cup	bananas, thinly sliced
1 cup	apples, diced
1 cup	pears, diced
½ cup	shredded coconut

Prepare fresh fruits. Mix all ingredients together. Chill before serving. Makes 10 servings, ½ cup each.

Waldorf Salad

2 cups	apples, very clean or peeled, and diced
¼ cup	dates, diced
1 cup	grapes, sliced in half

Dressing

1 tbsp.	lemon juice
1 tbsp.	oil
2 tbsp.	honey
¼ tsp.	nutmeg
¼ tsp.	cloves
⅛ tsp.	salt

Whisk dressing ingredients together. Add fruit and stir until well mixed.

Spinach Salad

6 cups	spinach
1 cup	mushrooms, sliced
¼ cup	bacon, crumbled
1	tomato, sliced or diced

Rinse spinach. Tear large leaves into bite-sized pieces. Place spinach, mushrooms, bacon, and tomato in a large bowl and toss immediately before serving. Serve with a vinaigrette or other dressing of your choice.

Jeannie's Cranberry Salad

2 lbs.	cranberries
2	apples
2	oranges
1 ½ cups	sugar

Using a food processor, grind fruits one by one. Do not peel oranges before grinding. Mix fruits and sugar and refrigerate several hours or overnight before serving. Makes 12 servings.

This salad is a wonderful fresh substitute for cranberry relish at Thanksgiving. If you like it a little more tart, use Granny Smith apples and cut the sugar back a little. For more texture, it is also nice to dice the apples rather than grinding them in the food processor.

Curry Dressing

1 tsp.	curry powder
¼ cup	oil
2 tbsp.	lime juice
2 tbsp.	apple cider vinegar
¼ tsp.	ginger
1 tsp.	salt
1 clove	garlic
2 tsp.	sugar

Whisk all ingredients together in a small bowl. Very good on diced, boiled potatoes, or used on a traditional green salad.

Taco Vinaigrette

Our friend Shawn loves this salad dressing. Whenever we get together for dinner, he always asks his wife, "Is Emily bringing that Taco Dressing?"

½ cup	oil
⅓ cup	apple cider vinegar
1 tbsp.	sugar
2 tsp.	chili powder
1 clove	garlic, pressed
½ tsp.	salt
¼ tsp.	black pepper
½ tsp.	cumin

Whisk all ingredients together. Serve on green salad.

Sweet and Sour Vinaigrette

¼ cup	oil
2 tbsp.	sugar
2 tbsp.	apple cider vinegar
1 tsp.	dried parsley
½ tsp.	salt
¼ tsp.	cayenne pepper

Whisk together in a small bowl. Use on Mandarin Chicken Salad or any other green salad.

Desserts

Desserts

Spice Cake

4 ½ cups	oat flour (see tip on page 3)
1 ½ cups	sugar
1 ½ tsp.	baking powder
½ tsp.	baking soda
1 tsp.	cinnamon
¼ tsp.	nutmeg
¼ tsp.	ground cloves
¼ tsp.	ginger
1 tbsp.	apple cider vinegar plus rice milk to total 1 cup
½ cup	oil
½ tsp.	vanilla

Combine flour, sugar, baking powder, baking soda, and spices. Add vinegar, milk, oil, and vanilla and mix well. Pour batter into a greased 9 x 13 pan.

Bake at 350°F for 35 minutes.

This cake is great served straight out of the pan, or frosted with orange or lemon frosting.

Chocolate Cupcakes

2 cups	oat flour (see tip on page 3)
1 cup	sugar
¼ cup	cocoa powder
1 tsp.	baking soda
½ tsp.	salt
⅓ cup	oil
1 tsp.	apple cider vinegar
½ tsp.	vanilla
1 cup	cold water

In one bowl, mix oat flour, sugar, cocoa powder, baking soda, and salt. In a second bowl, mix oil, vinegar, and vanilla. Pour cold water and oil mixture into dry ingredients and mix well.

Pour into lined muffin tins. Fill each muffin cup about ½ full.

Bake at 350°F for 20 minutes. These cupcakes are moist, so a toothpick inserted into a cupcake will have a few crumbs clinging to it.

Chocolate Snack Cake

Make Chocolate Cupcake batter as directed in the recipe above. Pour batter into a greased 8 x 8 pan and bake at 350°F for 25 to 30 minutes. This cake is moist, so a toothpick inserted into the cake will have a few crumbs clinging to it.

For a fancier cake, make a double recipe and pour batter into round cake pans lined with greased parchment paper. After baking, allow to cool for about 15 minutes in the pan and then carefully turn layers onto a cooling rack. After cooling completely, frost first layer with Chocolate Frosting, Creamy Frosting, or Peppermint Frosting. Place second layer on first layer and finish frosting.

Cinnamon Applesauce Cake

2 ½ cups	oat flour (see tip on page 3)
¾ cup	sugar
2 tsp.	baking powder
1 tbsp.	cinnamon
½ tsp.	baking soda
¼ tsp.	salt
1 cup	applesauce
2 tbsp.	oil
⅓ cup	rice milk
1 tbsp.	apple cider vinegar
	cinnamon sugar

Mix all ingredients with a spoon. Pour into a greased 9 x 9 pan. Shake cinnamon sugar all over the top of the batter.

Bake at 350°F for 30 minutes. Makes 9 to 12 delicious pieces.

This recipe started out as an attempt to make a cinnamon bread. After a few tries, I decided to add the applesauce. The resulting recipe was so sweet and yummy that we decided it should really be a cake. And so it is!

Fudge Brownies

½ cup	margarine or shortening (see tip on page *xii*)
1 cup	sugar
½ cup	cocoa powder
1 cup	oat flour (see tip on page 3)
¼ tsp.	baking soda
¼ cup	rice milk

Melt shortening or margarine. Mix in sugar. Add cocoa powder, oats, and baking soda and mix well. Add rice milk and mix well. Pour brownie batter into a 9x9 pan.

Bake at 350°F for 25 minutes.

Christina's Zucchini Brownies

2 ½ cups	oat flour (see tip on page 3)
1 ¼ cups	sugar
1 tsp.	salt
1 ½ tsp.	baking soda
¼ cup	cocoa
2 cups	grated zucchini (about 3-4 zucchini)
½ cup	oil
3 tsp.	vanilla

In a large bowl, mix together oat flour, sugar, salt, baking soda, and cocoa. In a separate bowl, mix the zucchini, oil and vanilla. Add the zucchini mix to the oat flour mix and stir well. Bake the brownies in an ungreased 9 x 13 pan at 350°F for 25 to 35 minutes or until an inserted toothpick comes out clean.

Frost with chocolate frosting or dust with powdered sugar for a fancier treat.

Blondies

1 cup	brown sugar
⅓ cup	margarine or shortening (*see* tip on page *xii*)
1 ½ tbsp.	rice milk
1 ½ cups	oat flour (see tip on page 3)
½ tsp.	baking powder
½ tsp.	baking soda
½ cup	chocolate chips

Heat brown sugar and margarine or shortening over medium heat until smooth. Remove from heat and mix in other ingredients except chocolate chips. Spread batter in greased 8 x 8 pan. Sprinkle chocolate chips on top.

Bake 35 minutes at 350°F.

If using chocolate chips, I recommend calling the manufacturer to double check for cross-contamination.

Baked Apples

A simple dessert that pleases those watching either the waistline or the sweet tooth.

4 large	Granny Smith apples
½ cup	chopped dried fruit, such as raisins or dates
2 tbsp.	brown sugar
½ tsp.	cinnamon
¼ tsp.	nutmeg
⅓ cup	apple juice

Wash and core the apples. Remove a little extra peeling from the top around the hole left by the core. Place the apples in an 8 x 8 baking dish.

Mix the dried fruit, sugar and spices and spoon ¼ of the mixture into each apple. Add the apple juice to the dish.

Bake at 350°F for 40 to 45 minutes, until the apples are tender. Every 15 minutes, pour some of the apple juice over the apples.

Fruit Crisp

4 cups	fresh sliced apples, peaches, or cherries
½ cup	oat flour (see tip on page 3)
½ cup	brown sugar
¼ cup	margarine or shortening (see tip on page *xii*)
1 tsp.	cinnamon
¼ tsp.	nutmeg
1 cup	oats

Put fruit in a pie plate.

In a bowl, mix all other ingredients with a pastry blender or fingertips until the mixture resembles coarse crumbs. Spread evenly over fruit.

Bake at 375°F for 30-40 minutes, until top begins to brown.

The fruit crisp can also be made with canned or frozen fruits. However, since canned and frozen fruits tend to be juicier, add ¼ cup instant tapioca to the fruit before sprinkling on the oat topping. While baking, the tapioca will soak up the extra liquid and thicken the fruit mixture.

Coconut Cookies

½ cup	margarine or shortening (see tip on page *xii*)
½ tsp.	vanilla
⅓ cup	lemon juice
¾ cup	white sugar
¾ cup	brown sugar
3 cups	oat flour (see tip on page 3)
½ tsp.	salt
½ tsp.	cinnamon
½ tsp.	soda
1 cup	coconut

With a mixer, mix margarine or shortening and lemon juice until smooth.

Add white sugar and brown sugar and mix until well blended. Mix in remaining ingredients. Form into 1 inch balls and place on cookie sheets.

Bake for 12 minutes at 350°F.

Oatmeal Cookie Cut-Outs

¾ cup	sugar
½ cup	margarine or shortening (see tip on page *xii*)
2 cups	oat flour (see tip on page 3)
1 tsp.	vanilla
½ tsp.	baking soda
½ tsp.	cream of tartar
¼ tsp.	salt
up to 2 tbsp.	rice milk

Mix sugar and margarine or shortening. Add remaining ingredients except for the rice milk and mix well.

Add a little rice milk at a time, adding only enough so that the dough forms into a ball when mixing.

Roll out to ⅛ to ¼ inch thick and cut with cookie cutters.

Bake at 350°F for 12 minutes.

After cooling, decorate with Creamy Frosting or Cookie Cutout Icing and sprinkles.

Oatmeal Cookies

We often customize these cookies by adding raisins or chocolate chips. My husband says that they are "dangerous," because he can't tell which one I've added until he tastes the dough. He prefers the chocolate chips.

½ cup	margarine or shortening (see tip on page *xii*)
1 cup	brown sugar
½ cup	white sugar
1 tsp.	vanilla
⅓ cup	rice milk
2 ½ cups	oat flour (see tip on page 3)
1 tsp.	cinnamon
½ tsp.	baking soda
¼ tsp.	salt
2 cups	old-fashioned oats
1 cup	raisins or chocolate chips, if desired (see tip on page 94)

With a mixer, mix the margarine or shortening and sugars. Add vanilla and rice milk and mix again. Add oat flour, cinnamon, baking soda, and salt and mix well.

Finally, stir in the old-fashioned oats (and chocolate chips or other additions, if you're customizing the cookies). Drop the dough by rounded tablespoons on the cookie sheet.

Bake at 350°F for 12 minutes. Makes about 4 dozen cookies.

Oatmeal Jammers

½ cup	margarine or shortening (see tip on page *xii*)
1 cup	brown sugar
¼ cup	rice milk
3 cups	oat flour (see tip on page 3)
½ tsp.	baking soda
½ tsp.	salt
⅓ cup	raspberry or other jam

With a mixer, first mix the margarine or shortening, brown sugar and rice milk. When that is well mixed, add the oat flour, baking soda and salt, and mix again.

One teaspoonful at a time, roll the cookie dough into balls.

Place the balls on a cookie sheet and use your finger to make an indentation in the top of each ball. Fill it with ¼ tsp. raspberry (or other favorite) jam.

Bake at 350°F for 12 minutes.

Chocolate Mint Cookies

¾ cup	margarine or shortening (see tip on page *xii*)
1 ½ cups	sugar
¼ cup	rice milk
½ tsp.	mint flavoring
2 ½ cups	oat flour (see tip on page 3)
½ cup	cocoa
½ tsp.	baking soda
½ tsp.	salt

Mix margarine or shortening and sugar. Add rice milk and mint flavoring and mix well. Add oat flour, cocoa, baking soda and salt. Drop by tablespoons onto a cookie sheet.

Bake at 350°F for 12 minutes.

Oil-based candy flavorings are likely to be free of allergens. Stores that carry cake decorating supplies usually carry this type of flavoring. Alternately, use 15 to 20 starlight mints, crushed, or 15 to 20 mint leaves, chopped in a blender, to flavor the cookies.

Fudge Cookies

¾ cup	margarine or shortening (see tip on page *xii*)
1 ½ cups	sugar
¼ cup	rice milk
2 ½ cups	oat flour (see tip on page 3)
½ cup	cocoa
½ tsp.	baking soda
½ tsp.	salt

Mix margarine or shortening and sugar. Add rice milk and mix. Add oat flour, cocoa, baking soda and salt. Drop by tablespoons onto a cookie sheet.

Bake at 350°F for 12 minutes.

Fudge Sandwich Cookies

Make one recipe of Fudge Cookies. Instead of dropping on the cookie sheet, roll into equal-sized balls and place on the cookie sheet. After baking and cooling completely, frost bottom of one cookie and place another on top of frosting. Delicious with Creamy Frosting, Chocolate Frosting, or Peppermint Frosting.

Fudge sandwich cookies have become so popular around our house that my family no longer requests the chocolate cookies. They just ask for the ones with frosting.

Fudgy Thumbprint Cookies

You can use any kind of jam in these chocolaty cookies, but our favorites are strawberry or raspberry. Any kind of fruit that tastes good dipped in chocolate would work well in this cookie.

¼ cup	margarine or shortening (see tip on page *xii*)
¾ cup	sugar
¼ cup	rice milk
2 cups	oat flour (see tip on page 3)
¼ cup	cocoa
¼ tsp.	soda
½ tsp.	salt
⅓ cup	jam

Mix margarine or shortening. and sugar with a mixer. Add rice milk and mix for one minute. Add oat flour, cocoa, soda, and salt and mix well. Roll dough into balls about 1 inch in diameter. Press your thumb or finger into the center of each ball to make a small depression and spoon ¼ tsp. of jam into each depression.

Bake at 350°F for 12 minutes. Allow the cookies to cool on the cookie rack for 1 or 2 minutes before moving to a rack to cool completely.

Stovetop Chocolate Cookies

½ cup	margarine or shortening (see tip on page *xii*)
1 ½ cups	white sugar
⅓ cup	cocoa powder
½ cup	rice milk
¼ tsp.	salt
3 cups	quick or whole oats
1 cup	flaked or shredded coconut

Prepare a place to drop cookies after they are cooked by spreading aluminum foil or waxed paper on 2 cookie sheets or on an equivalent amount of counter space.

Place margarine or shortening, sugar, cocoa powder and rice milk in a sauce pan. Cook and stir over medium heat until the mixture begins to bubble and is well blended. Cook and stir for 1 minute more. Remove your pan from the heat. Sprinkle the salt over your mixture and then stir in. Stir in the oats and coconut.

Drop oat mixture by rounded tablespoonfuls onto the waxed paper or foil. Allow the cookies to cool until they are easy to handle, and enjoy!

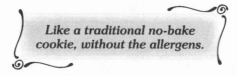

Like a traditional no-bake cookie, without the allergens.

Ginger Apricot Cookies

Ginger Apricot Cookies are moist, slightly chewy, and have a fresh, distinct flavor. If you find the ginger a little too overwhelming, you can reduce it or eliminate it altogether, but it is lovely with the apricots.

½ cup	margarine or shortening (see tip on page *xii*)
1 cup	white sugar
¼ cup	lemon juice
2 ½ cups	oat flour (see tip on page 3)
½ tsp.	baking soda
½ tsp.	salt
½ tsp.	ginger
1 cup	finely chopped dried apricots

Beat margarine or shortening and sugar. Add lemon juice and mix well.

Mix in oat flour, baking soda, salt, and ginger. Add apricots and mix well. Drop by tablespoons onto a cookie sheet.

Bake at 350°F for 12 minutes.

Gingerbread Cookies

4 cups	oat flour (see tip on page 3)
½ cup	white sugar
1 tsp.	baking powder
½ tsp.	baking soda
1 tsp.	ginger
½ tsp.	cinnamon
½ tsp.	cloves
¼ cup	margarine or shortening (see tip on page *xii*)
½ cup	molasses
1 tbsp.	apple cider vinegar

With a mixer, mix oat flour, sugar, baking powder, baking soda, and spices until blended.

Add margarine or shortening, molasses, and vinegar and mix well. The dough should form a ball while mixing.

Roll the cookie dough onto a floured or non-stick surface with a rolling pin. Roll out about ¼ of the cookie dough at a time. Try to roll it to a thickness of about ¼ inch.

Using cookie cutters, cut gingerbread dough into your chosen shapes. Move to cookie sheets.

Bake at 375°F for 7 minutes. Before removing cookies from the cookie sheet, allow them to cool for about 1 minute. This recipe makes about 30 gingerbread men.

Fancy Lemon Sandwich Cookies

These are my mother's favorites. The first time she tried them, she grinned and said, "I don't think ANYONE could find anything wrong with these cookies!"

Cookies:

1 cup	margarine or shortening (see tip on page *xii*)
2 cups	white sugar
½ cup	lemon juice
5 cups	oat flour (see tip on page 3)
1 tsp.	baking soda
1 tsp.	salt

Beat margarine or shortening and sugar. Add lemon juice and mix well. Mix in oat flour, baking soda, and salt. Shape small balls of cookies dough. Balls should be the same size.

Bake at 350°F for 12 minutes. While cookies are cooling, make frosting.

Frosting:

¼ cup	margarine or shortening (see tip on page *xii*)
1 ½ cups	powdered sugar
2 tbsp.	lemon juice
3 tsp.	lemon zest

Beat margarine or shortening. Add ½ of the powdered sugar. Add lemon juice and lemon zest. Mix in remaining powdered sugar.

When cookies are completely cool, spread frosting on one cookie and top with a second cookie. Repeat until all cookies are made into sandwiches.

Fruit-Filled Cookie Bars

If you use a really sweet jam, such as raspberry, these will be very sweet as written. If you use a less sweet jam, like sour plum or orange marmalade, you may want to experiment with the amount of sugar to find a combination that you really like.

1 cup	oat flour (see tip on page 3)
1 ¼ cups	quick oats
⅓ cup	brown sugar
¼ tsp.	baking soda
⅓ cup	margarine or shortening (see tip on page *xii*)
8 oz.	jam

Combine oat flour, oats, sugar, and baking soda. Cut in margarine or shortening until mixture is evenly combined.

Remove ⅔ cup of oat mixture for topping. Press remainder of the mixture into the bottom of a 9 x 9 pan. Spread jam over oat mixture.

Sprinkle the ⅔ cup oat mixture on top of jam.

Bake at 350°F for 35 minutes. Allow to cool completely (1 ½ to 2 hours before cutting into bars.

Pumpkin Pie Morsels

⅓ cup	margarine or shortening (see tip on page *xii*)
1 ½ cups	oat flour (see tip on page 3)
½ cup	brown sugar
1 cup	canned pumpkin
1 tsp.	apple cider vinegar
½ tsp.	allspice
½ tsp.	cinnamon
½ tsp.	nutmeg
1 tsp.	baking powder
¼ tsp.	salt

Beat margarine or shortening with a mixer until soft. Add oat flour and sugar and mix well. Add remaining ingredients and mix again. Drop with a spoon onto a cookie sheet.

Bake at 375°F for 12 minutes. Frost with citrus frosting after cookies are cool.

These have a really nice fall flavor, but are great any time of year. Thanks to canned pumpkin, they are available year-round!

Chocolate Marshmallow Cookies

½ cup	margarine or shortening (see tip on page *xii*)
1 ¼ cups	sugar
¼ cup	rice milk
2 ½ cups	oat flour (see tip on page 3)
½ cup	cocoa powder
½ tsp.	baking soda
½ tsp.	salt
	miniature marshmallows

Beat margarine or shortening until soft. Add the sugar and mix well. Add the rice milk and mix again. Finally, add the oat flour, cocoa powder, baking soda, and salt. Mix well.

Using about 1 tablespoon of dough, flatten the dough in your palm and place 4 miniature marshmallows in the dough. Wrap the cookie dough around the marshmallows. Repeat this procedure until all the dough is used.

Bake cookies at 350°F for 12 minutes.

Creamy Frosting

¼ cup	margarine or shortening (see tip on page *xii*)
up to 2 cups	powdered sugar
2 tbsp.	rice milk
1 tsp.	vanilla extract
or ¼ tsp.	oil-based candy flavoring

Beat margarine or shortening with a mixer. Add ½ cup of the powdered sugar and mix well.

Add rice milk and vanilla and mix until smooth. Add enough of remaining powdered sugar to make the frosting a good consistency for spreading.

This makes enough frosting to frost one small single layer cake or 12 cupcakes.

This frosting is great for anything; frosting a cake, making sandwich cookies, topping cupcakes—use your imagination!

Citrus Frosting

¼ cup	margarine or shortening (see tip on page *xii*)
up to 2 cups	powdered sugar
2 tbsp.	lemon juice or orange juice
2 tsp.	lemon or orange zest

Beat margarine or shortening with a mixer. Add ½ cup of the powdered sugar and mix well.

Add juice and mix until smooth. Add enough of remaining powdered sugar to make the frosting a good consistency for spreading.

This makes enough frosting to frost one small single layer cake or 12 cupcakes.

Chocolate Frosting

¼ cup	margarine or shortening (see tip on page *xii*)
¼ cup	cocoa powder
up to 2 cups	powdered sugar
3 tbsp.	rice milk
1 tsp.	vanilla extract

Beat margarine or shortening and cocoa powder together. Add milk and vanilla.

Add enough of remaining powdered sugar to make the frosting a good consistency for spreading.

Makes enough frosting to frost a small single layer cake or 12 cupcakes.

Peppermint Frosting

¼ cup	margarine or shortening (see tip on page *xii*)
20	peppermint candies, crushed
up to 4 cups	powdered sugar
¼ cup	rice milk

Beat margarine or shortening, crushed peppermint candies, and 1 cup of the powdered sugar together.

Add milk and remaining powdered sugar alternately until most of the powdered sugar is blended in and frosting is a good spreading consistency.

Makes enough frosting for a 2 layer cake or 24 cupcakes.

This frosting is delicious between fudge cookies or on chocolate cake.

Cookie Cutout Icing

This frosting will harden so that cookies can be stacked together without sticking. It will really come in handy any time you need to send cookies somewhere—as a school treat, on someone's doorstep at Christmas, or even in a container in your pantry.

1 cup	powdered sugar
2-4 tsp.	rice milk or juice
2 tsp.	light corn syrup
	food coloring

Mix powdered sugar and rice milk or juice. Add corn syrup and mix well. Add food coloring. Spread over cookies and allow to set.

Index

Index

2004712

Made in the USA